So Loved

beyond

your

wildest

dreams

D1363739

GREGORY DICKOW

So Loved
Beyond Your Wildest Dreams

Printed in the United States of America

For information, please write

Gregory Dickow Ministries
PO Box 7000
Chicago, IL 60680

or visit us online at www.gregorydickow.org.

Table of Contents

Chapter One

Get Swept Away

Love is invincible facing danger and death.
Passion laughs at the terrors of hell.
The fire of love stops at nothing—
it sweeps everything before it.
Flood waters can't drown love,
torrents of rain can't put it out.

—Song of Solomon 8:7, Message

God's love is a BEAUTIFUL DISASTER. When it hits you, it changes everything. Listen to Solomon's description more closely—It's invincible. God's love laughs at terror. It stops at nothing, and nothing can stop it. WOW! That's what I'm talking about. That's what God feels toward you.

It sweeps everything before it. God's love sweeps away:

. . . our sin,

. . . our loneliness,

. . . our pain, and

. . . our fears.

When the love of God hits you the way that I'm praying it will, nothing will remain the same!

God's Love Is Going to Wreck You.

It's going to wreck your old fears and limitations. It's going to wreck your old view of yourself and others. It's going to sweep you off of your feet and take you to a place that you've never been before.

God's love comes in like a storm in our lives . . . not to hurt us, but to blow away what has been hurting us; to destroy what is destroying us; and to bring disaster to what has been bringing disaster to us all our lives.

God comes with a vengeance, but His vengeance is not against you. It's against the things that are hurting you.

God takes vengeance out on fear. He takes His vengeance on anxiety, sickness, and lack. He takes His vengeance on anything that tries to hurt His beloved children—everything that has ever tried to get between you and Him.

Do you want an encounter with God like that? Do you want a Christianity like that—a Christianity that is so full of love and power that it changes you; so full of goodness and mercy that follows you, seeks you, and chases you down?

You see, we don't have to chase God. His love is so great that He's the one who chases us.

The prodigal son's father didn't wait for his son to get all the way home. As soon as he saw a glimpse of his son out of the corner of his eye, far off in the distance, Luke 15:20 says, " . . . he ran to his son, threw his arms around him, and kissed him continually" (Luke 15:20).

That's aggressive, invincible, tornado love! That's the love of God. The father didn't wait for the son to clean up his act, change his clothes, or become a servant. The son just turned toward his father, and the father came running, chasing, embracing, kissing, blessing, and healing!

God Is Chasing You Down with His Goodness and Love.

The bride in Song of Solomon 2:16 says, "My lover is mine and I am his." We belong to each other. When you discover that this is the kind of relationship God wants to have with you, it changes how you look at yourself, how you look at Him, and how you look at others. You are no longer alone in this fight to try to conquer life and conquer sin. You are ONE WITH HIM. He is yours, and you are His. This love relationship conquers all. This love never fails. This love gives you purpose, meaning, and reason to live. It gives you something to look forward to, every day of your life.

You Are Significant.

All the temptations of the enemy are temptations to doubt God's love for us. When the devil tempted Jesus in the wilderness, he said, "Throw yourself down from here.

Your angels will catch you" (Luke 4:9, Matthew 4:6). And Jesus answered, "It is said: 'Do not put the Lord your God to the test'" (Luke 4:12).

What Jesus was saying at that point was, in essence, "I won't throw myself down, because God loves me too much. He has a plan for my life, and there's too much to live for. I am not going to kill myself, because God's love for me is too great, and His purpose for me is too great. I am too significant to Him, too important to Him, and too valuable to Him." And so are you!

You see, the temptation to give up or give in went away when Jesus reminded Himself and the enemy that the Father loved Him too much to let him throw his life away. And that's exactly how God feels about you!

Say to yourself, "I will not accuse myself because of low value or low self-worth. I am worth everything God paid for me. He wouldn't have bought me with His blood if He didn't love me. He wouldn't have bought me with His blood if He didn't value me. He wouldn't have bought me with His blood if He didn't think I was significant to Him."

God didn't send Jesus to die for what was insignificant . . . He died because YOU ARE SIGNIFICANT TO HIM!

That's the kind of love that sweeps away all sin, loneliness, temptation, pain, and fear. That's His fierce, passionate, tornado love. Get ready to be swept away!

God's love sweeps away three things:

1. Our sin. "I've swept away your sins like a dark cloud." (Isaiah 44:22). The English phrase, *dark cloud*, comes from the Hebrew for *hanging cloud*. It sweeps away what is hanging over you and blocking your view of His love. God's love sweeps away the things reminding you of your past.

2. Our desires. Something changes when we discover His love. "I have loved you with an everlasting love, drawn you with loving kindness" (Jeremiah 31:3). He never gives up on you, but He also never forces you to obey Him. But that love is so strong that it sweeps away all of our wrong desires and our other ambitions.

3. Our fears. God's love for us is relentless. It pursues us continually. It leaves no doubt how immense and intense it is. When you discover His love, you'll have faith, not fear. You'll be confident because everything's going to be all right.

Chapter Two

So Loved

God knows you completely, He understands you completely, and He loves you completely. That's why you can go to Him with anything you are struggling with.

God knows the way you think and why you think it. He knows your feelings, your flaw, your deepest secrets, and deepest desires, and He still loves you.

When you understand God's love for you, it's easy to trust Him. So many people have a hard time believing God and believing God's promises, but that's because faith works by love (Galatians 5:6). It's not our love that causes faith to work, but it's understanding God's love for us that makes it *easy* to believe His promises.

If a *stranger* made a promise to you, you might be skeptical. If *someone you love* makes a promise to you, you hope you can believe it. But if *someone who loves you and died for you* makes a promise, you can be absolutely certain that He will keep His promise. You see? Love is driven to keep its promise, and this love empowers us to believe. The deeper your understanding of His love, the higher your faith will rise!

Dare to trust God today. Believe His love, and you will trust Him as you never have before. God has prepared a way for you. What He has prepared for you is beyond what you can imagine right now. It's more beautiful than you can imagine. He will take you higher and farther than you've ever gone before.

His love is deeper than we will ever understand, but let's try to understand it better today, because the deeper you understand His love, the more secure and confident you become, and the higher you will dream His dreams.

If you could see God right now, you would see that His eyes are full of love, not wrath. Your fears and feelings of inferiority would drop off of you like a shabby old coat you've been desperate to throw away. You are clothed with something greater than words can describe, clothed on the inside with a warmth and feeling that is undeniable and indescribable: the love of God.

Yes, I know love is a choice, a decision, and a commitment, but it starts as a feeling. God *feels* love for you, and He wants you to feel it today! It's what leads us to Him.

He says, "I have loved you with an everlasting love; therefore I have drawn you with My lovingkindness" (Jeremiah 31:3).

God doesn't draw us through fear of punishment or wrath. He doesn't draw us by dangling the reality of hell over us. He draws us by his love.

Hell is real, but that's why He came: to seek and save the lost, to save us from being separated from Him forever. If you lose something that you don't care about, you forget about it. But if you lose something you care deeply about, you search and search until you find it. That's what God does for you. He loves you so much that even when you were lost, He came to find you, save you, and bring you home. This kind of relentless, furious love amazes me and makes me want to please Him more.

Jesus describes His love for us when He talks about Solomon and his bride. "You have made my heart beat faster, my sister, my bride; You have made my heart beat faster with a single glance of your eyes, with a single strand of your necklace" (Song of Solomon 4:9).

Why would God love us so? This is a mystery. But His heart is full, His mind is brilliant, and yet you make His heart beat faster. I know that is hard to grasp, but I am asking the Holy Spirit to reveal it to you today, "that you may be able to comprehend what is the breadth and length and depth and height; to know the love of God which surpasses knowledge" (Ephesians 3:18–19).

I like how the Message translation says it: that you would experience, "the extravagant dimensions of Christ's love. Reach out and experience the breadth! Test its length! Plumb the depths! Rise to the heights! Live full lives, full in the fullness of God."

You see, this is the secret to the full life—the life God intended for you. Notice, because of the understanding of this love, what God can do.

"God can do anything, you know—far more than you could ever imagine or guess or request in your wildest dreams!" (Ephesians 3:20)

Are you ready for God to exceed your wildest dreams? Well, it starts by having some wild dreams! And God is going to give them to you.

Chapter 3

Healing the Human Heart

But before we dive into your **wildest dreams,** let's look at how God brings them to pass.

Jesus wants you to experience God's dream and destiny for your life. But to do so, we have to give some attention to your heart.

The heart is the manufacturing center of our dreams, hopes and desires. Solomon said, "Watch over your heart, for from it flow *the issues, desires, and harvests* of your life" (Proverbs 4:23).

Because the heart is the container of our dreams and desires, the enemy works to damage, break, and disappoint our hearts.

This is why Jesus says that He came to heal the brokenhearted. Our hearts break because of betrayal, disappointment, and rejection. Broken dreams are the result of a broken heart. You're capable of big dreams, but the heart must be healed.

As Jesus stepped into His ministry, He said, "The Spirit of the Lord is upon me because He has anointed me to preach the Gospel to the poor . . ." (Luke 4:18). This is the most important thing. His first assignment is to bring you the Good News, win you to the Father, bring you into relationship with God, and introduce you to His saving grace.

But then, once we receive the Gospel, His very next mission is: "To heal the broken-hearted." There's so much more God wants to do in each of our lives, beyond saving us. This is so important, because (as I described earlier) the heart contains our dreams and hopes. It is the manufacturing center of all dreams, thoughts, and prayers (Proverbs 4:23).

God doesn't put a hope or desire in your head only; He puts it in your heart also. A broken heart cannot contain the dreams, hopes, destinies, and the greatest things God created us for. If the heart is broken, the dreams spill out.

For this reason, Paul writes, "Eye has not seen, ear has not heard, nor has it entered the heart of man the things God has prepared for those that love Him" (1 Corinthians 2:9). The things he describes are infinitely beyond our highest hopes, prayers, dreams, thoughts, and desires (Ephesians 3:20).

God has prepared amazing things for you: the greatest life and the greatest things you can imagine, both in this life and in the life to come. But with a broken heart, you can't be impregnated with the dream long enough to carry it to full term.

As a result of a broken heart, most people are not living the dream that God created them for. When the heart is broken, we keep attempting to fill an empty heart with things that dull our pain or occupy our attention.

For the young, it's easy to dream. When we are young, girls dream of being ballerinas, and boys dream of being astronauts. Life is all about imagining and dreaming. But somewhere along the line, our heart gets broken, and we shut down our *dream center* within.

We get disappoint or experience a broken relationship, we get hurt and rejected, and we get affected by our mistakes— and so our dreams diminish. We begin to think so much smaller, because we don't want to get hurt or disappointed again. As we get older, we realize life hurts, and we experience more pain and damage, so we lower our expectations of ourselves, people, and God.

God wants to heal the heart, so He can awaken the dream. That's why God sends His Spirit to us. Romans 5:5 says, "Hope does not disappoint, because the LOVE OF GOD has been POURED into our hearts by the Holy Spirit."

The Holy Spirit's first assignment in our lives is to reveal to us the LOVE OF GOD. Then, once we are secure in God's love, He comes upon us, and, "your sons and daughters shall prophesy. Your young men will see visions; and your old will dream dreams!" (Acts 2:17)

When He pours His love *within* us by the Holy Spirit, He then awakens within us His visions and dreams!

Hope (dreams and desires) cannot disappoint, BECAUSE THE LOVE OF GOD IS POURED OUT WITHIN YOU, BY THE HOLY SPIRIT.

Our hopes and dreams will go unfulfilled when our heart is broken by disappointment, betrayal, or regret.

"Now hope does not disappoint . . ." (Romans 5:5). We disappoint ourselves, but hope never disappoints.

People are going to disappoint you. But your dreams, hopes, and desires will not disappoint you, because the love of God has been poured out in our hearts. The Holy Spirit has been given to us. He's a gift (Acts 1:4). All you do is receive. That's when hope will soar again.

Paul doesn't tell us that the Holy Spirit has been sprinkled on us with a mist or a morning dew. We understand the difference between a *pouring* and *sprinkling*. When it's pouring, you walk out of your car, and you're instantly drenched. This is the kind of love Paul is talking about—pouring, drenching love! This is the kind of love that gives you the power to see your highest dreams, thoughts, and prayers realized—infinitely beyond.

So today ask the Holy Spirit to reveal God's love to you in a supernatural way and to heal you today of disappointment, broken hopes, and shattered dreams. Invite the Holy Spirit to heal any brokenness of heart.

NOW let's dream again!

Chapter Four

Love Makes You Dream

"Now Jacob loved Joseph more than all his children" (Genesis 37:3). "And Joseph dreamed a dream" (Genesis 37:5). Notice the correlation between these verses.

Here is an Old Testament picture of New Testament love. Jacob symbolizes our heavenly Father, and Joseph represents us. God loves *you* more than anything. Jacob loved Joseph so much that he gave him something: a coat of many colors. You see? Love always gives. Love is always accompanied with a gift, a demonstration of love. The most well-known verse in the Bible, says GOD SO LOVED the world that He gave His only begotten Son" (John 3:16).

GOD SO LOVED that He gave.

Jacob so loves Joseph that he gives him this amazing coat. The coat represents two things in the Bible: righteousness and authority. This is a royal coat. There are many colors, many blessings, and manifestations of this coat. It means his father prizes his son. What does it mean for us? It means we're loved, and we're prized.

When you think something is really valuable, you pay the highest price. God sees you with such great value that He paid for you with His own blood.

"To Him who loved us and washed us from our sins in His own blood, and has made us kings and priests to His God and Father, to Him be glory and dominion forever and ever. Amen" (Revelation 1:5–6).

Notice the order of what God did: God loved us, THEN He washed us, and THEN He made us kings and priests. He did not love what was washed; He washed what He loved. He loved you as you were but didn't leave you as you were! Then He made us kings and priests—giving us royal position and authority in Christ. He gives us the coat of righteousness and authority.

This royalty destroys inferiority. When you know you're loved and that you are a king and priest in Him, you stop seeing yourself small and limited. You see yourself seated with Christ (Ephesians 2:6). And when you see yourself like this, you think at a higher level and dream at a higher level.

The deeper your sense of God's love, the higher you dream His dreams.

Let's see how this plays out in Joseph's life. **In Genesis 37:3, Jacob loves Joseph. Then, in Genesis 37:5, Joseph dreams a dream.** This is not a coincidence. When we know we're loved by our Father, we begin to dream. When we doubt His love, we live at a low level, just trying to survive, living day-to-day, grinding out an existence; constantly looking for someone in life to validate or approve of us; constantly searching for significance and satisfaction, but never finding it. But when we know we're loved by our Father, we are no longer living lowly, waiting for the scraps from the Master's table. Our sense of approval and acceptance by our heavenly Father lifts us from low self-worth, and small thoughts and dreams. We begin to think the highest thoughts and dream the highest dreams!

"Joseph dreamed a dream. And when he told it to his brothers, they hated him even more" (Genesis 37:5).

Notice two things here:

1. His father's love caused him to dream God's dream.

2. And his father's love prepared him from his brothers' hate.

Haters hate dreamers, but they can't stop God's dream for your life, no matter what they do to you. God's love will always triumph over people's hate.

This love empowered Joseph to dream and to endure the opposition to his dream. God's dream and plan for you is so much bigger than you could imagine. You're going to live at a higher level—these hopes and dreams will not be disappointed, because the love of God has drenched you with relentless, unstoppable love.

God is saying: "I love you so much, so I'm giving you my covering, my authority and my dream. I'm giving you everything you need." Start seeing God's love that way, and you will be unstoppable.

God always loves you first, because His love powers you through the trial, the betrayal of others, and the opposition you will face.

"Now Joseph had been taken down to Egypt . . . The Lord was with Joseph, and he was a successful man" (Genesis 39:1,2). Even in the pit, we become successful and elevated when we know God's love. Even when it seems like our God-given dreams are delayed, they will never be denied when we know God's love.

Let's return for a moment to Jesus' baptism to see how this played out in His life. After Jesus arose out of the waters, He hears a voice from heaven: "You are my dearly loved Son, and you bring me great joy" (Mark 1:11 NLT).

Now consider for a moment, that Jesus hadn't done a miracle yet; preached a sermon, fed a multitude, or died for our sins. Before Jesus had done one thing FOR God, He receives this one thing FROM God: "You're my dearly loved son." This is what prepares Jesus for the wilderness and the temptation, and ushers Him into His calling. Notice the very next verse: "And immediately the Spirit compelled him to go into the wilderness where He was tempted . . ." (Mark 1:12–13).

Jesus could handle the temptation He faced because of the love of the Father (Mark 1:11–14). Then He began to preach the good news. He was powered through temptation and powered into His purpose by the love of the Father! And you will be, too. 1 John 4:17 says, "As He is, so are we in this life."

The purpose and dream for your life flows from God's love for you.

Joseph was hated by his brothers. They left him in a pit, and then sold him into slavery. Joseph was falsely accused, thrown into prison, and left to die. But . . . Jacob loved Joseph, and Joseph dreamed a dream!

Joseph's father's love powered him through his persecution and pain. When your awareness of your Father's love never dies, your dream never dies.

Isn't it interesting that only after being stripped of his coat, thrown into a pit, and sold into slavery is Joseph referred to in the Bible as "a prosperous man." (Genesis 39:2). Another translation says, "a successful man."

Why would God wait until Joseph was stripped of EVERYTHING in his life before he finally called him a prosperous man? He had lost his possessions, his position, his relationships, his home, and everything he had. Then, and only then, God called him a prosperous man. Why?

Because when you have nothing except the presence of God's love, you have everything. Even when you've been stripped of everything, you can't be stripped of God's love. It has been poured into your heart. They can take your coat, trash your name, and try to step on your dream, but they can't get the love of God out of your heart. God put it there. He is madly in love with you, and that's going to get you through whatever you're facing today.

William Cullen Bryant's great poem, "The Battlefield," goes:

> Truth, crushed to earth, shall rise again;
>
> The eternal years of God are hers;
>
> But Error, wounded, writhes in pain,
>
> And dies among its worshippers.

Just as truth crushed to earth shall rise again, so will your dream and destiny. It doesn't matter how much adversity life or the enemy bring. Your dream will rise because it came from God.

Joseph's dream was birthed by love, and love never fails.

Meditate on God's love for you. Expect His power, and you will walk in your God-given purpose.

Chapter Five

Dream Thieves

Is there something significant that you are hoping for?

A dream in your heart? For your life? Marriage? For your children? For your future? Has He shown you what on Earth you are here for?

I heard the Lord speak to me recently, saying, "Tell My people there are some thieves trying to steal their dreams and rob them of their destiny."

It's time to expose the dream thieves that are trying to rob you of your destiny and God's dream for your life.

God DOES have a dream for you, and it's A DREAM BEYOND YOUR WILDEST IMAGINATION. But you need to understand that before your dream can become a reality, YOU MUST CLOSE THE DOOR TO THE DREAM THIEVES.

There was a woman whose home was broken into, and thieves stole her most valuable possessions. She filed a police report, and the insurance company came and approved replacing all of her stuff. She thought all was restored and well.

But only a few weeks later, her home was robbed again! And—you guessed it—the same thieves came and took the new replacements.

When she called the police again, they said, "Well, ma'am, this is common. You see, when a thief discovers an access point into your house, he will often come again to see if that access point still remains. If you haven't sealed off the window or other access points that the thief used, he will keep coming back UNTIL YOU CLOSE OFF THE ACCESS POINT."

Many times we open doors—THE THIEF'S POINT OF ACCESS—into our lives. And until the access is closed off, the dream thieves can come back and steal from us time and time again.

This first dream thief is: doubting God's love for you!

God's love is the gateway to God's dream and destiny for your life. We've illustrated this through Joseph's life and through Jesus' life, and its the secret to living a life beyond your wildest dreams.

Satan comes to steal that knowledge of God's love for you—to convince you that God's just putting up with you, that He's mad at you for some reason, that He's against you or doesn't approve of you; and that you haven't done enough. The enemy wants you to think, "I've fallen too far. I've made too many mistakes. I'm not good enough for God to love me. I don't deserve God's dream for me."

But these are all lies from the devil. God's love for you never decreases. God said, "I love you with an everlasting love" (Jeremiah 31:3). There's nothing you can do to change God's everlasting love for you.

When you have confidence in His love for you, it casts out fear. And when you have no fear, Satan has no access.

The second dream thief is: believing that people can control the outcome of our lives.

Satan uses people to get at us. Sometimes he uses your coworkers, your friends, your relatives, and even the people who are closest to you. It's nothing new today! Look at what happened to Joseph.

"Now when they saw him afar off, even before he came near them, they conspired against him to kill him. Then they said to one another, 'Look, this dreamer is coming! Come therefore, let us now kill him and cast him into some pit'" (Genesis 37:18–20).

Can you imagine anyone, let alone your brothers, hating your dream so much that the devil would use them to try to kill it—and you? But we need to realize something: Whatever they did TO Joseph was no match for what God would do FOR Joseph. If God is for you, who can be against you?

No person, no human being on the face of this Earth, can stop the purpose and destiny God has for you.

As I said earlier, haters hate dreamers, but they can't stop God's dream for your life. Forgive them and keep moving forward. Put your faith in God's promises. He's watching over His Word to perform it.

So the thief comes to steal your dream by stealing the Word about God's love for you. And that's why we need to treasure His Word in our heart (Psalm 119:11). It will stop these dream thieves from robbing us of our destiny.

Jacob's love for Joseph prepared him for what he was about to go through. God's love for you will do the same! If Satan can't shatter your concept of God's love, he can't shatter your dreams.

Now, let's get to know His love better.

Chapter Six

His Love Is Better than Wine!

"Let Him kiss me with the kisses of His mouth, for your love is BETTER than wine" (Song of Solomon 1:2).

Medically speaking, wine has been known to have some interesting health benefits when used in moderation. According to many medical studies, wine can lower your cholesterol, protect your heart with antioxidants, control blood sugar, boost your immune system, affect your brain positively, keep your memory healthy and sharp, help fight off a cold, help fight cancer, and help you get slimmer. What a list! *This is NOT meant to be an argument for drinking wine,* but to point out that if those are some of the benefits of wine in moderation, and His love is BETTER than wine, then we can start expecting some great things in our lives as we drink freely from His love.

When something is better, it can at least do what the other thing can do AND THEN SOME. If wine can do all those things above, then God's love can do far BETTER than that. If we can tap into this pure love, we won't need any substitutes!

When a person is drunk, they forget their past, their mistakes, and their inhibitions. They're bolder and will do things they wouldn't normally. But God's love is better than that. His love gives you the boldness to pray for the sick and see them healed, the boldness to tell somebody about the Jesus that saved your life, and the boldness to command demons to flee!

Before I knew Jesus and the love of God, by the time I was just 17, I was getting drunk and high on drugs every day. I was addicted! But I wasn't just addicted to the THC chemical or the alcohol content. I was addicted to feeling better for a moment. I was addicted to having peace, and forgetting how lonely I was. I was addicted to feeling good. Ultimately, the addictions were broken in my life—not because I had strong willpower or therapy, but because I found something better. It's not because I'm so holy that I'm not addicted to those substances anymore. I simply found something better. His love is better than wine!

The prostitute is not a prostitute because she's more evil than you are. She wants and needs love, even if but for a moment. To feel valuable enough to get a couple hundred bucks, she's willing to sell a piece of herself. She simply hasn't discovered the love that's better than wine.

Sometimes I think God saved me when He did, because He knew I would have gone even further over the edge than that prostitute did. We were rescued by God's love. We were swept up. We were the kid in the pig pen, the prodigal son, and the Father ran to us. It wasn't our holiness or morality that brought us back to the Father. It was His mercy that drew us.

God's peace, freedom, deliverance, and love are better than wine, better than alcohol, better than any substance that temporarily dulls our pain. God's love doesn't just temporarily dull pain; it heals our pain.

A priest named Father O'Malley was pulled over. He rolls down his window and the officer smells liquor on the priest's breath and sees an empty wine bottle in the back of the car. "Have you been drinking, Father?" "Only water," the priest replied. The officer asked, "Then what is that bottle of wine in the back of your car if you're only drinking water?" The priest looked at the bottle, then looked up to heaven and said: "Good Lord, You've done it again!" Now, even though Jesus did turn water into wine once, He wants to give you something even better!

Why is God's love better than wine? (Song 1:2b)

1. It can be taken and enjoyed without question. You can drink freely of God's love without question. There are always questions about wine. Some will tell you to abstain. Others will say it's okay to drink it freely. A third group will say, use it in moderation. So there's a question about how much wine a person should allow himself. But God's love is better, because you can drink it without measure, without having to wonder "Have I had too much?" "Am I going overboard here?" There is no overboard. Drink freely, continually, and consistently of His love, and of His Spirit!

2. You can have it without money. His love is limitless. It's free. Isaiah 55:1 says, "Drink freely and buy wine from me without cost." I've counseled many people who have lost fortunes because of their addiction to alcohol, drugs, gambling, or some other habit. Enjoying this Christian life doesn't cost you anything, but it cost Jesus everything. That addictive life, that source of temporary pleasure costs you much. But God's joy, peace, and love cost you nothing. You can drink and drink, and God never makes you pay the bill. His drinks of love and goodness are always ON THE HOUSE!

3. God's love never turns sour. Wine can't do the job completely. It can make you feel good for a short period, but it's not a lasting high. God's love is everlasting, and it never turns sour. God never turns on you. Alcohol can make you happy for a moment and then turn you into a raging maniac. The more you understand God's love, the more joyful, happy, and peaceful you'll be.

4. God's love has no side effects. The alcohol and drugs in this world have side effects. One is getting sick, another is feeling empty afterwards, another side effect of getting wasted, is feeling regret. God's love has no bad side effects. It has good ones! It makes our faith work. It wins others to Him. And it heals!

The Healing Properties of Love

In addition to the many physical and emotional effects that love has on us, here's a great example:

Some years ago psychologist Dr. Karl Menninger, noting the cause of his patients sicknesses and mental illnesses called for a critical step in the plan for them. He said, "In this clinic we will create an atmosphere of creative love." All patients were given large quantities of love; no unloving attitude was to be displayed. At the end of six months the time spent by patients in the institution, compared to others, was cut in half.

"How beautiful is your love, my sister, my spouse! How much better than wine is your love, and the scent of your perfumes than all spices!" (Song of Solomon 4:10) Wow, Jesus is now saying to you: how beautiful is your love. He calls you His spouse.

This is the most unfathomable topic we could ever discuss. Not only are we blown away by His beauty, He's blown away by ours. He sees you as the beautiful bride He created you to be. When God looks at you, He sees you like Jesus. It's a mystery: God is our father, yet Jesus is our spouse. It's the best of all relationships. He's the best of what any father, husband, brother, or friend could be to you. And at various times in our lives, we need Him to be each of those things to us.

When you discover the love of God, He gives you the perfection you could never get from another person. There are imperfections within even the best of relationships. You can never have perfect love—a love so deep it casts fear completely out of your life. No matter how much a man loves his wife, he cannot cast out all her fears, heal her insecurities, or completely satisfy the loneliness and emptiness inside her. God gifts us with imperfect relationships so we will always be aware of our need for Him.

When you taste His love, it makes you a better person, because you're no longer trying to meet the needs, fill the voids, and heal the hurts with this world's provision. You have been healed and satisfied by the love of Jesus and no longer put a demand on people to give you something you were designed to only receive from Him.

Most people don't see God like this. I pray the veil will be removed and we no longer see a God of religion, but the God of mercy, compassion, and grace—the God who is love.

Chapter Seven

Divine Love

God's love meets every need. God SO LOVED the world that He gave His Son and everything else we would ever need!

"He that did not spare His own Son but delivered Him up for us all . . . how shall He not also with Him, freely give us all things" (Romans 8:32). God's not holding anything back from you. That's divine love.

We live in a world of conditional love. Human love is the love of the lovely. "I love you because you're beautiful, handsome, or rich. I love you because you have something for me, because you're appealing to me."

But where does that leave the rest of us? We don't look like this world's models, spend like their CEOs, or perform like their athletes. The rest of us don't fit in that category of the elite of the elite. Our deficiencies prevent the "loveliest people" to love us. But we don't need that shallow human love. God's love isn't like that. He doesn't love what is lovely. God makes lovely what He loves. His love transforms you into the person you had always hoped you would be.

We cannot earn God's love or approval. Remember, in Mark 1:11, Jesus came up out of the waters of baptism and heard the voice of God saying, "You are my beloved Son, and in you I am well-pleased." He had not yet raised the dead, fed the multitudes, walked on water, or set anybody free. This is divine love. There's nothing you have to do earn it, deserve it, or produce it.

God's love heals everything in our lives. Every problem we have comes down to three primary forces: Fear, loneliness, and self-hatred. Perfect love deals with these things. **It starts by casting out fear.** It's easy to fear that if you don't get it all right, if you don't get it all together, you're going to disappoint God, or His feelings for you will change. But PERFECT love casts out this fear. You can rest in His love. You can have faith in this love that never fails and never fails you.

Self-hatred. This is looking in the mirror and seeing somebody you don't like, noticing what you don't like more than what God says about you. But God loves you just the way you are. He doesn't leave you the way you are, but He loves you deeply. And this unconditional love will heal you of self-hatred.

God's love also deals with **loneliness.** Mother Teresa said, "Loneliness and the feeling of being unwanted is the most terrible poverty." Perhaps you felt there's a hole in your heart. God's presence and His love deliver us from loneliness and fill that emptiness in our lives. Then He connects us to people in a church that should become a spiritual family.

I heard about a marine that got saved and his experience as a new Christian. The power of God hit him, and he stopped drinking, chasing women, and getting into trouble. But something still troubled him. He approached his pastor with sadness, confessing, "I don't miss any of my old lifestyle, but the one thing I miss is the fellowship at the tavern—laughs, stories, and beers. I haven't found anything like it. I got nobody to admit my faults to, to put their arm around me and tell me I'm still okay." We sure don't want to hear that as pastors. We want to know that our churches are the real thing and are meeting the deep needs people have. But that often is not the case.

The local bar has become somewhat of a counterfeit for the fellowship and love that God wants us to experience with Him and with His people. A neighborhood bar serves liquor instead of Scripture, giving an escape rather than bringing people into a reality. But it welcomes any type of person. You can't shock anybody in the bar with your mess. You can tell somebody a secret, and they'll honor the code (or be so drunk that they forget.) Tell somebody a secret at church, and before you know it, everyone knows. Why is it that sometimes people can find more safety in a bar, celebrate more "cheers" in a bar than in church? Maybe you remember the theme song from the television show, "Cheers." "Be glad there's one place in the world where everybody knows your name, and they're always glad you came. You want to go where people know, people are all the same . . . where everybody knows your name."

The church is supposed to be that place! But our leaders have let us down, not because their motive is bad or they lack theology. They're often professional speakers and organizational leaders, but perhaps they lack the encounter with God's love that transforms them in a deep way. Or perhaps they're afraid to delve deep into a discovery of this kind of love and share it with people, because they're afraid it will be too soft and make it too easy for people to sin. But people sin no matter how easy or hard preachers make it. I'm convinced that the more we truly uncover and reveal the depths of God's love to people, the LESS they'll sin. Luke 7:47 says, when we realize we are forgiven of much, we love much. We all need forgiveness, but those who REALIZE how forgiven they are will love more. And obedience to God becomes the REFLEX to God's love. His love hits you in the right spot, and the natural reaction we have is obedience, not disobedience. That's what Jesus meant when He said, "If you love me, you'll obey me." That wasn't a threatening or demanding statement. He was stating the natural fact. Love causes a reaction of honor and obedience to God.

The church is supposed to be the place where that fountain of love is always flowing—the place where people could come and feel such love, safety and acceptance that they never have to go to a bar again. A place where you can be honest and not judged, but instead be healed. I want you to know the riches of His love so deep that it touches you in places that no human could ever touch. That's the love of Jesus Christ.

In God's family, relationships transcend status, race, ethnic group, background, money, and education. It's the love of God given to people born of the same heavenly Father. It doesn't matter if you're black or white, Irish or Italian, Puerto Rican or Mexican. This kind of brotherly affection breaks down every barrier.

That's what the body of Christ can be when we get swept away by this love and ask God to let it affect us deeply until it shows up in every relationship we have, every worship service we experience, and everywhere we go.

This world doesn't know this kind of love. What this world desperately needs is an oasis in the desert place of loneliness and disconnection—a group of people who truly love each other; a place where they can connect with God and with people who will help them on their journey; a place of healing, hope, and real change. That's God's dream for every church: that when you come in, you would taste something so good that you never want to settle for anything less.

Chapter Eight

The Greatest Love of All

In the French Revolution, a young man was condemned to be killed at the guillotine.

He was loved by many, but no one could do anything to help—except one man, who loved him more than all the others put together.

It was his father! When the lists were called, the father—*whose name was exactly the same as the son's*—jumped in front of his son, answering to the name. As he rode into the gloomy place of execution, his head rolled beneath the axe instead of his son's—the sacrifice of a father's mighty love.

What a picture of Christ's love for us. That he would take our name—the name of Man—and become the victim of mighty love for us!

His Love Is Unparalleled.

"Greater love hath no man than this, that a man lay down his life for his friends" (John 15:13).

A British publication once offered a prize for the best definition of a friend. Among the thousands of answers received were the following:

"One who multiplies joys, divides grief, and whose honesty is inviolable."

"One who understands our silence."

"A watch that beats true for all time and never runs down."

But the winning definition read: "A friend is the one who comes in when the whole world has gone out." (Bits and Pieces, July, 1991).

Jesus is the friend that comes in when the whole world has gone out! He sticks closer than a brother (Proverbs 18:24).

He not only loves us; He wants us!

Jesus desires you! "I am my beloved's, and my beloved is mine" (Song 6:3). He's wants you. He loves you. He cares about you. He's crazy about you. We're not misfits to God. We're not the leftovers. He has such adoration and affection for you—not puppy love, infatuation that wears off. He doesn't love you reluctantly out of duty. He loves YOU because He is love, and because He sees what's lovely inside of you even when you don't. His love for you is immeasurable. Its unstoppable!

Genesis 29:20 says that Jacob loved Rachel so much that he served seven years for her, and they seemed to him but a few days. Jesus laid His life down, died on the cross, because of how much He loves you. That's the kind of love that marks you forever—that He would go through all of that—for you!

Remember, the love of God has been POURED out into your heart by the Holy Spirit. Ask God to awaken you to this mighty love. It will complete you, heal you, and fill you with joy.

Chapter Nine

Pure Joy

" . . . Love is invincible facing danger and death. Passion laughs at the terrors of hell. The fire of love stops at nothing—it sweeps everything before it. Flood waters can't drown love, torrents of rain can't put it out. Love can't be bought, love can't be sold—it's not to be found in the marketplace."

—Song of Solomon 8:6–7, Message

The love of God is invincible. "Yet in all these things we are more than conquerors through Him who loved us" (Romans 8:37). God's love can't be stopped, defeated, overwhelmed, overtaken, or ruled out. There is no law against it. The force of love stops at nothing. It keeps driving away your past, worries, fears. It sweeps away everything before it—demons, difficulties, weaknesses, shortcomings, failure, and disappointment.

We don't need as Christians to get our brooms out, focused on trying to fix everything in our lives. What we need to do is discover the breadth and depth of the love of God and it will sweep everything before it.

The first manifestation of really getting and understanding the love of God is JOY. Galatians 5:22 says,

"The fruit of the Spirit is love." When you discover the love that is truly God-breathed, Spirit-birthed love, you don't have to do anything in exchange.

Pure joy is knowing you're loved with no conditions. He loves you in spite of your flaws, not when you clean up your act.

Pure joy starts with the Good News. "The angels said to them, 'Do not be afraid. I bring you GOOD NEWS that will cause great joy'" (Luke 2:10 NIV). How can you not be afraid? Perfect love. "There is no fear in love; but perfect love casts out fear" (1 John 4:18). There's nothing like hearing good news when you're going through a bad day!

Pure joy comes from victory. After Tiger Woods won his first tournament after a two-year drought years ago, the 72nd tournament win of his career, when they put the microphone in front of him, they asked, "How does it feel?" The two words that came out of his mouth without hesitation were "Pure joy." Victory brings pure joy. We can have joy today because we're more than conquerors through Him Who LOVES US! (Romans 8:37–39)

Jesus wants you to know you have the victory, and to "Be of good cheer," because He has overcome the world. Jesus conquered sin, and we get to enjoy the gift of righteousness.

Jesus conquered the curse; we get to enjoy the blessing. He did all the heavy lifting; we get to enjoy the victory.

Pure joy comes from believing what you have not seen (1 Peter 1:8). "Though you have not seen him, you love Him, you rejoice with joy inexpressible and unspeakable." Thousands have met the love of their life online. They fell in love with mere words. It's possible to love somebody just because of the words they say and the pictures they paint with those words. If a person can have feelings for a person they've never physically met before, how much more can we have feelings for God? Because we have felt His impact.

Unspeakable in the Greek language is translated as, "unable to find expression in words." Jesus is too wonderful for words. He truly is "a gift too wonderful for words" (2 Corinthians 9:15 NLT). This is why we worship. It's only in the shallow streams of water that the sunlight shines on the pebbles. But in the ocean, the depth is too dark and has never been searched with light. If you don't have difficulty describing God's love, you haven't discovered it yet. It's so deep that it's hard to find expression for at times. I could search throughout eternity and never find this love that makes no record of wrong, that is patient and kind. It bears all things, believes all things, endures all things, hopes all things. It never fails, fades out—it is the most unfathomable love and when you discover it, it brings pure joy. If it's not hard for you to describe it, ask God to help you discover it.

Pure joy comes from finding what has been lost in your life (Luke 15).

A shepherd leaves 99 sheep to find one. "Come rejoice with me."

A woman loses one of her ten coins. When she find it she says, "Come over and rejoice with me." All the angels in heaven rejoice when one person is saved. He loves us so much that He wants us to be in His family. We should rejoice because He wants us so much.

The father of the prodigal son went running to the son. "This son of mine was dead. Let's celebrate. We've got to party!" That's what God is saying. He doesn't care about all that's been wasted. His son was back where he belonged. When you are connected to the Father, pure joy is restored.

Chapter Ten

God's Not Mad at You
He's Mad About You!

A while back, I read a headline in the New York Post—"God Hates Us!" I was reminded of how so many people actually do feel that way when something bad happens in their life. Such was the case with the children of Israel in Deuteronomy 1:27, when they said, "Because the Lord hates us, He has left us to die in the wilderness." Of course God did not hate them at all, but their distorted view of God shaped their beliefs and decisions just as it does for everyone. That's why we need to KNOW how much He loves us, no matter what we go through. This is the number-one problem in the world: a distorted view of God. Many people think God is a God of wrath and judgement. And while He is just and righteous, He poured out His wrath on Jesus. Anyone who receives Jesus as Savior is delivered from the wrath of justice.

But even His wrath is based on His love. Because He loves us, He is willing to pour out the judgement we deserve on His own Son. He loves you that much! As I have said many times, God's not mad at you; He's mad about you. He's crazy about you!

Jesus knew this, as we have seen in Mark 1:11, when we hear the first recorded words from God to Jesus. Before He ever DID anything for God, He heard these words: "You are My Beloved Son, in whom I am well pleased!" The assurance of being loved was what empowered Jesus to fulfill God's purpose for His life—as it will you as well. We need to learn to *be-loved*—to *be* who God created us to *be*. As a result, we will *do* what God intended us to do.

Jesus obliterated religion! In this one moment, He crushes the performance-oriented Christianity. He proves that God loves us freely; that we don't have to do for Him to receive from Him.

First, the Father gives Jesus His seal of approval. ("You're My beloved Son, in you I am well-pleased".) THEN, Jesus is launched into fulfilling His ministry. He shows us that BEING loved is the secret to DOING love—and doing what we're called to do.

We've had it backward. Religion does not liberate; it oppresses. It strikes at the heart of God.

Do you see why religion is such a slander at the nature and character of God? Our stupid lists of do's and don'ts and rules is just a religious attempt to earn God's love. It's pointing an arrow at the heart of God, saying, "You don't love me yet, but I'll make You love me. Watch me perform; watch me sacrifice and pray and obey and keep my lists of do's and don'ts—That ought to make You love me! I'll prove my significance by making myself good enough for You to love."

This is manipulation. This is how twisted religion is— it insidiously inspires us to try to control God with our actions.

If our do's and don'ts would get God to love us or bless us, then it would be a form of manipulation. And God won't be manipulated. He simply wants to be believed. He wants you to believe the love He has for you and therefore dare to trust Him.

But unmerited love and grace—ah, that's God saying: "YOU DON'T HAVE TO IMPRESS ME. I LOVE YOU. I ACCEPT YOU. I CHOOSE YOU. I BLESS YOU!"

Consider for a moment that we are called human "beings," not human "doings." In other words, just "being" is enough to deserve God's love. We don't have to *do* something to get it.

This means that *no matter what you've done or what has been done to you; no matter who you are,* **YOU ARE LOVED— accepted and treasured by God.**

This is the good news, the Gospel of Jesus Christ, the heart and soul of a satisfied life.

We are the beloved of God.

God is saying, "You are mine. You are special to Me."
This love has no conditions attached to it. Love is His
unbreakable promise. It means: "I will never break my
promise. I will never bring up your sins again. And I will
never leave you or forsake you."

Yet it often seems that everything people do is motivated
by the idea of gaining somebody's love—in the form of
approval or attention.

Especially in our search for relationships, we try to buy
love, earn it, trade for it, or seduce it—going to any lengths
to win it with gifts, money, or promises. We'll even adver-
tise for it online—though it may still elude our grasp.

Others already in intimate relationships may still be
yearning for love anyway. A woman I read about put it
this way: "I've only been married six months, but I feel
completely alone —that I don't matter, like a puppy sitting
under the table begging for scraps, looking for some sign
that he still loves me. I know I am pathetic to need this,
and hate it."

What would make a woman feel so empty and worth-
less? It's that desperate craving for love, so strong that,
like the song, we're sometimes "lookin' for love in all the
wrong places."

DIVINE LOVE, unlike the deficiency of human love, leaves us with no scar. It heals us everywhere we hurt. Why? Because God accepts us as we are, embracing us in His loving arms, and never letting go.

Friend, when you realize you are God's beloved—with the deepest conviction—your life is going to change in amazing ways. Studies have shown that increased doses of love decreased stress levels, elevated overall emotional contentment and improved physical health.

The Five Secrets to Discovering God's Love

But for now, if you're hurting or doubting God's love, first and foremost, here's how to turn it around.

1. DISPEL THE MYTH OF AN ANGRY GOD. As I mentioned earlier, the first generation of the children of Israel believed that God was mad at them—that He hated them. So as a result of their skepticism and negative beliefs, they failed to experience the fullness of His blessing. In our own lives, we sometimes mistakenly view God as punishing us for our mistakes and flaws rather than as an all-forgiving, all-loving presence in our lives. I tell people all the time, "God is not mad AT you, He's mad ABOUT you. He *IS* love. Love gives. Love understands. Love never fails. That's the kind of God I'm talking about!"

2. TALK TO GOD. Pour your heart out to God, telling Him all that is in you, until there is nothing left to tell. Nothing you tell Him is going to knock Him off the throne! He is patient, compassionate, and understanding—the greatest shoulder to cry on, and the mightiest counselor! *And*—He doesn't charge $200 per hour for His therapy! So hide nothing. Bare your soul to the One who will not judge or reject you. He knows your greatest fears and human failings, and no matter what you say, you remain His beloved. You will feel His love washing over you, like the powerful refreshing waves of the sea.

3. GIVE UP PERFECTIONISM. Let go of the pursuit altogether. Be loved the way you are. You don't have to have it "all together" to be loved. Nobody does. We all have things about ourselves that we'd like to change or improve, that we're dissatisfied with. But you don't have to fix everything wrong in your life in order to be loved. Realize that God doesn't change you to love you. He loves you—and His unconditional acceptance is the catalyst for positive change in your life. So relax—for works of art take time. When you accept this truth, follow it up by being patient with yourself. I like the poem that goes: "It took God a week to make the Earth and stars, the Sun, the Moon, Jupiter and Mars. How very special I must be—'cause He's still workin' on me!"

4. BANISH THE VOICES OF REJECTION. Remember: You are the crown of His creation—His beloved. As such, you were made with a unique purpose that no one can fulfill but you. For this reason, you are important to God and to His world. What others may reject or turn away, God accepts and embraces. Look in the mirror and tell yourself that you are chosen by God. See the good in your reflection—your strengths, your special qualities, the energy in your eyes, the beauty in your presence.

5. ASK GOD TO HEAL YOU. Many of us have suffered the wounds of rejection, abandonment, abuse, or mistreatment. Left behind are wounds and scars. We all have them. Perhaps you've been through a difficult divorce or have experienced some sort of betrayal. Maybe you feel consumed with worry and guilt. Ask God to let you know *His* love; to let you see the wonders of all that He has for you. Ask Him to heal you from the memories preventing you from believing in His love. Pray a simple prayer like this: "Lord, I want to feel your love and your warm embrace. Heal me from the memories that have blocked my ability to experience your love. Set me free to know I am your beloved today. Amen."

Chapter Eleven

A Daily Declaration of God's Love

I want to leave you with this daily declaration, because I know how powerful meditating on God's love can be. Take the next 30 days or longer and simply start each day declaring this out loud. It will change your outlook on life and your "inlook" on yourself!

"I will greet this day with God's love in my heart! It is the greatest secret to success no matter what life brings. It calms every storm. When the enemy persecutes my soul, love comforts it. When I face darkness, love brings light. When my heart is overwhelmed, love will inspire and encourage it! When my heart is distressed, love will remind me of God's goodness over the years."

"When I feel discouraged, love will lift my hands to the Lord and fill my mouth with a song. I will worship Him this day with His love in my heart."

"I will greet this day with God's love in my heart! When it feels like heaven is silent, love will remind me that God knows what I'm going through. He has a plan. And He will provide for my every need."

"I will greet this day with God's love in my heart! Love will lead me. Love will direct me. Love will inspire me. Love will heal me. Love will fill me. Love will revive me. "

"I will greet this day with God's love in my heart! Love will deliver me from my enemies. It will protect me in times of storm. Because of God's love today, all those who seek to hurt me will be stopped, for love makes my shield of faith work."

I will love all that I come in contact with today. I will love the weak and make them strong. I will love the inspired and be inspired by them. I will love the empty and help them be filled. I will love the filled, and they will overflow! I will love the broken, and they will be healed."

"I will greet this day with God's love in my heart, and it will quench all the darts of the wicked one. I will confront everyone I face, with love. It will shine through my eyes, bring a smile to my face; and bring waves of peace through my voice. It will lower people's defenses and empower them to experience God's presence!

I will greet this day with God's love in my heart! Because He loves me, I will love myself. I will love others. And I will love life, no matter what I face! From this moment forward, fear and hate leave my body and my mind. Fear and hate leave my family and my home, in Jesus' Name!"

Receive the Gift
of Salvation

Perhaps you have never received Jesus Christ as your Savior and Lord, or you're not sure you will go to heaven when you die. Well, you can be sure today.

Or perhaps you have tried to be good, and you thought, "If I am good enough, if I go to church or try to clean up my life, then I will be saved." But none of that will save you. There is only one way to get to heaven—by accepting forgiveness and the gift of salvation, through the sacrifice Jesus made on the Cross.

I want to lead you in this prayer of faith, and something miraculous is going to happen in your heart.

Pray this out loud:

"Heavenly Father, I accept Jesus Christ into my life as my Savior and Lord. I believe Jesus died for my sins and rose from the dead. I receive the forgiveness of my sins through the blood of Jesus. Take out my old heart, Lord, and give me a new heart and a new life. Make me born again. By grace I am saved today through faith. I freely accept your love and grace to enable me to walk with you all the days of my life, in Jesus' Name. Amen!"

Now listen. That is just the beginning.

God wants you to grow. He wants you to move forward and live in His purpose for your life. When we get born again, we start a brand-new life. You don't have to live like you used to live. But we all need help to live out this new life in Christ. If you have just received Jesus as your Savior and Lord, contact our prayer center at 847-645-9700 and let us know. I want to help you.

Next Steps

Read the Bible and talk to God. God has a great plan for your life. He loves you and wants the best for you. You are His child now. You are in the family of God today. Your life will never be the same again!

Now thank Him for making you His child. And don't doubt! You are a child of God right now! John 1:12 says, "To as many as received Jesus, to them He gave the right to become sons and daughters of God."

Next, you should find a good Bible-believing church, where you can grow together with other believers and find your place in a spiritual home! It is my pleasure to welcome you into the family of God!

The Baptism in the Holy Spirit

The baptism in the Holy Spirit is an empowering for service that takes place in the life of the Christian (Acts 1:5,8). In it, we are immersed in the Spirit's life and power. To illustrate, if we drank water from a glass, then the water would be inside of us. However, if we went to the beach and stepped into the ocean, then we would be in the water. We receive, as it were, a drink of the Holy Spirit when we are saved, but when we are baptized in the Spirit, it is as if that initial drink becomes an ocean that completely surrounds us. Just as the indwelling Spirit that Christians receive when they are saved reproduces the life of Jesus, so the outpoured, or baptizing Spirit reproduces the ministry of Jesus, including miracles and healings.

Why Do We Need the Baptism in the Holy Spirit? We need a power beyond ourselves for service and ministry in Christ's Kingdom. When Jesus gave the Great Commission (Matthew 28:19–20), He knew that His disciples could not fulfill it in their own power. Therefore, He had a special gift in store for them: It was His plan to give them the same power that He had—the power of the Spirit of God.

So, immediately after giving them the Great Commission, Jesus commanded His disciples not to leave Jerusalem, but to wait for what the Father promised, "which," He said, "you heard of from Me; for John baptized with water, but you shall be baptized with the Holy Spirit not many days from now" (Acts 1:4–5) He further promised, "You shall receive power when the Holy Spirit has come upon you; and you shall be My witnesses both in Jerusalem, and in all Judea and Samaria, and even to the remotest part of the earth" (Acts 1:8).

The disciples gathered, and "suddenly there came from heaven a noise like a violent, rushing wind, and it filled the whole house where they were sitting. And there appeared to them tongues as of fire distributing themselves, and they rested on each one of them. And they were filled with the Holy Spirit and began to speak with other tongues, as the Spirit was giving them utterance" (Acts 2:3,4).

Then Peter explained to the crowd that gathered that they were seeing the working of God's Spirit and told them about Jesus. This is the same gift that God wants for you!

How Do I Receive the Baptism in the Holy Spirit? First, once you have accepted Jesus Christ as your Savior you simply ask God to baptize you in the Holy Spirit. The Bible says, "Ask, and it shall be given to you" (Luke 11:9). Second, believe you have in fact received this gift from God. The apostle Paul, said, "Did you receive the Spirit by the works of the law, or by hearing with faith?" (Galatians 3:2). The answer, obviously, is faith. You have to believe that if you ask, you will receive. Pray this prayer if you desire to receive the baptism in God's Holy Spirit:

"Heavenly Father, at this moment I come to You. I thank You that Jesus saved me. Baptize me now in the Holy Spirit. I receive the baptism in the Holy Spirit right now by faith in Your Word. And right now I receive the gift of speaking in other tongues. May I be empowered to serve you in a new dimension from this day forward. Thank You, Father, for baptizing me in Your Holy Spirit. Amen."

Now, having asked and received, begin to practice the power of the Spirit. An ideal place to begin is where the first apostles did, praising God in your brand-new tongue. To do this, begin praising God out loud in whatever words God brings to you by the Spirit's inspiration. Tell Him how much you love Him. Thank Him, worship Him, and yield your voice to Him. Now let Him give you new words of praise you never heard before. Praise Him with those words, too. You'll find that this can be a very rewarding experience of communication with God that will build up your faith. Continue to pray to God each day in the language that the Holy Spirit has given you.

If you have more questions about the Holy Spirit and His gifts, contact our Prayer Center at 847-645-9700, so we can pray with you according to God's Word.